No Problem!®

How to focus on solutions

E. M. Hanley

Livre

Livre Publishing (Pty Ltd)
www.noproblembook.com

Hanley, E. M. (Elizabeth M.)
No problem!: how to focus on solutions
Bibliography.
Includes index.
ISBN 978-0-615-63499-9

Published 2012 US edition.

Disclaimer
The material contained in this publication is intended to provide readers with information about health. However the publication does not provide medical advice or prescribe the use of any technique as a substitute for professional treatment of physical or mental problems. The author and publisher make no representations regarding the contents of this publication. They expressly disclaim any warranties as to the accuracy or completeness of the information contained in this publication and accept no responsibility for any errors or omissions.

A Good Book

At times it gathers dust on a table or
in a bookcase, given thought by no one.

Come a time, however, of loneliness,
of sadness, of boredom, of need to escape,
of anxiety about the future and this
faithful friend casts off its
dust and unfolds ...

St John Bosco

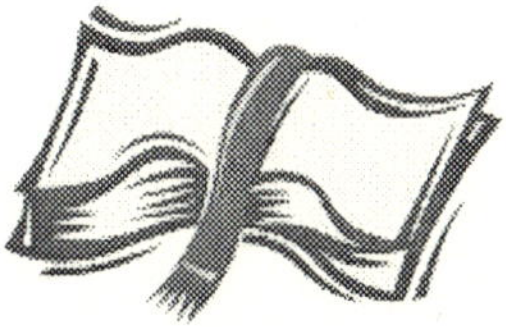

To my husband
John
everyday is a blessing

'Your task is to build a better world,' God said.

And I answered, 'How? This world is so big and complicated. I am so small. There's nothing I can do!'

And God, in all his wisdom said, 'Let me help you build a better you.'

Author Unknown

Enjoy a No Problem! life

CONTENTS

Introduction

Part 1 The Problem

Part 2 The Solution

CHAPTER 1

Four Simple Tips

Living a great life is what we all want, yet problems can keep us stuck in a rut.

> We find ourselves 'living to survive' instead of 'living to thrive'.

Wouldn't it be great if every time you ran into a problem you could just say 'No Problem! I can handle this' and feel sure that things would be OK.

Read on and you will find 'easy to use' and 'easy to understand' information that helps you focus on solutions – and enjoy a No Problem! life.

No Problem! reviews and explains in simple terms what the best-selling self-help authors say about problem solving. Authors such as 'Dr Phil' McGraw, Anthony Robbins, Stephen Covey, Susan Jeffers, Dale Carnegie, M. Scott Peck and many more.

I have grouped their advice under four simple tips so that you will be able to easily recall their words of wisdom.

On the pages that follow these tips will help you embrace that No Problem! feeling when things go wrong. It includes real life examples that show you how these tips can work in your life.

What most people don't realize is that:

> You do not react to the events in your life – you react to your thinking about the event.

When your thinking about an event is negative, then your negative thinking can upset you and keep you stuck in a problem. Even after an event has past negative thinking may still be affecting you.

You don't have to believe every negative thought that pops into your head. You can choose your thoughts. You can choose helpful thoughts. Say to yourself: *It will be OK, I can handle this.*

> Your power lies in changing your thinking. When you change the words you are saying to yourself - your feelings about the problem will change.

Helpful thinking will give you the strength to deal with any problem. When you are strong on the inside, problems will not bring you down.

Using the **four simple tips** helps you move from negative thinking to helpful thinking more quickly and easily – so you can focus on solutions.

The four simple tips that guide you to solutions:

1. Define – see it as it is, not worse than it is
2. Own – take control and feel the power
3. Truth – face the truth to see solutions
4. Balance – check the bigger picture

You don't have to make big changes. Making even a small effort to use the tips will make big differences to your life.

Enjoy a No Problem! life

Part 1 explains how the four simple tips help you focus on solutions. Use any one of the tips and you will improve your problem solving ability. **Using all four tips will lead you to solutions.**

Part 2 is the Problem Solving Guide. It guides you step-by-step in applying the four simple tips to any personal problem you may be struggling with. **The guide contains powerful questions that will help shift your focus onto solutions.**

CHAPTER 2

Focus on Solutions

I DID NOT EXPECT THAT!

Each time you get into your car to go somewhere there are thousands of people driving on the roads with you. What are the chances someone is going to make a mistake? The chances are very high. Just think of how many times you've made mistakes behind the wheel.

Now think of a time when someone else made a mistake driving. Did you swear and beep at them and wonder how they got their license? Let's get real! How could mistakes not happen with so many people on the road? It is inevitable, someone is going to make a mistake. We all make mistakes.

You need to expect problems when driving and you need to expect problems in your life. Problems are going to happen; the question is – how are you going to react to them?

Say to yourself each morning:

I expect problems, but it will be OK. I am going to focus on solutions. I can handle any problem.

EXPECT PROBLEMS

In one of the best-selling self-help books of our time, M. Scott Peck's *The Road Less Traveled,* Peck opens our eyes to expecting problems.

Peck writes, 'life is a series of problems'. He explains that when you truly understand this, when you truly see this and expect problems, then problems will not have such a negative effect on you.

When you don't expect problems,
it's much harder to deal with them.
Your negative thinking can be
overwhelming and hard to manage.
Your focus remains stuck on the problem.

When you expect problems,
it reduces their negative power over
you and your negative thinking is
easier to manage. You will be able
to more easily shift your focus to solutions.

Now that you know problems are headed your way, also know that the *four simple tips* help you move from problems to solutions faster.

FOCUS ON SOLUTIONS

Focusing on solutions is the key to problem solving. While this is easy to say, it's not always easy to do. Problems, especially difficult ones, can throw us into a negative state of mind.

Your negative thinking will stop you from focusing on solutions.

It is natural to feel upset when problems arise. We all fall victim to, and struggle with, negative thoughts. But the longer you remain in a negative state of mind, the harder it is to focus on solutions.

Ask yourself:
'Am I stuck in negative thinking?'

Read on and you will learn how to 'thought break' so negative thinking won't overwhelm you. You will see how easy it is to focus on solutions by using the four simple tips.

ha ha ha, ho ho ho, ha ha ha, ho ho ho, ha ha ha, ho ho ho, ha ha ha, ho ho, ha

A Chuckle a Day Keeps the Doctor Away

Jokes have been included in each chapter to remind you that laughing daily is essential for a healthy life. Despite having problems, you can actively seek to laugh.

Laughter is like internal jogging.
Laughter gives you relief from stress.
Laughter strengthens your immune system.

Create happiness yourself...
Don't wait for someone else
to make you feel happy.

- Regularly watch a funny TV show or movie.
- Cut out jokes or cartoons and stick them up.
- Find humor in ordinary everyday things.
- Think of an amusing moment and talk about it.
- Play with your kids or your pets. Be a kid.
- Act silly with your partner. When you are happy it will rub off on them.

ha ha ha, ho ho ho, ha ha ha, ho ho ho, ha ha ha, ho ho ho, ha ha ha, ho ho, ha

PART 1

THE PROBLEM

Two lawyers - one married, one single - won a multi-million dollar payout for a client. Their client was so happy, he treated them to a weekend at a five-star golf resort. The married lawyer did not want to take his wife along so he told her she couldn't come. His wife was very upset that he would go away without her.

The first afternoon, the two lawyers had just finished a great round of golf and were sitting at the bar drinking cocktails. The concierge came up to the married lawyer and handed him a blank envelope.

'That's strange, there's nothing written on it,' said the single lawyer. 'Who do you think it's from?'

The married lawyer tore open the envelope and unfolded a piece of paper that was inside. When he realized that it too was blank, he shook his head and grimaced.

'What's the matter?' the single lawyer asked. 'It's from my wife,' replied the married lawyer. 'She isn't talking to me!'

CHAPTER 3

Houston, We Have a Problem

[see page 104 for the solution]

Journey of a Lifetime

When a space shuttle rockets off the launch pad, NASA Control Center at Houston doesn't know how the 'space journey' will go. But what they do know is that there will be problems. They know that it is not a matter of if, but of when they will hear the message, 'Houston, we have a problem'. Given that problems are guaranteed, NASA has in place established strategies to follow, allowing them the best chance to deal effectively with any problem that may arise, therefore giving the astronauts the best possible 'space journey'.

As it is with your life, you do not know how your 'life journey' will go, but what you do know for sure is that you will have problems. Like NASA Control Center, you can better deal with problems if you have an established strategy – four simple tips – in place. You will be ready to respond to any problem and work toward solutions, so that you can continue to give yourself the best possible 'life journey'.

Types of Problems

Knowing what type your problem is will lead you to solutions faster.

While on the outside problems can be very different in appearance, looking inside they are remarkably similar.

In his best-seller, *The 7 Habits of Highly Effective People*, Stephen Covey explains that problems can be categorized into one of three areas:

- Direct control problems
- Indirect control problems
- No control problems

When you know the type your problem is, you can see how much control you have over it and what you need to do to work towards a solution.

Direct control problems

These are problems that involve your own behavior over which you have direct control, such as negative thinking, temper flare-ups, unhappiness, fear, depression, bad habits, addictions, procrastination.

Indirect control problems

These are problems that involve another person's behavior over which you have limited control, such as an angry partner, a misbehaving child, a rebellious teenager, a difficult boss, an annoying friend.

No control problems

These are problems that you have no control over, such as the past or world events, for example your childhood, earthquakes, storms, serious illness.

Think of a problem in your life today. What type is it?

Use Your Influence

Direct control problems

You have the most influence and control over direct problems. You can solve them by working on yourself, that is by changing your thinking and behavior.

> With some problems you may need help to change your thinking or behavior. Only you can make that choice. For example getting help to quit smoking or drinking.

Indirect control problems

You have limited influence over indirect problems as these involve other people's behavior.

> Covey explains that you cannot change another person, you can only influence them through changing yourself.

Change yourself so you can cope with people who won't change. For example deciding to walk away and calm down instead of arguing.

Covey's motto for *indirect control* problems is:
Seek to first understand ... then to be understood.
This will improve your influence.

No control problems

You have no influence over no control problems. You need to accept and learn to live with them. Covey warns that such problems can keep you stuck in concern. To avoid living in concern or worry you need to change the way you think.

> Covey remarks that *no control* problems can only be overcome by seeking to *change your thinking*. For example deciding to let go and stop dwelling on the past.

With any problem you encounter the only aspect of the problem you can control is you.

Covey provides a powerful insight into problem solving. He explains that solutions come from *using your influence*. Covey's message is both revealing and empowering, as he writes:

> 'Whether a problem is direct, indirect, or no control, we have in our hands the first step to the solution. Changing our habits, changing our methods of influence and changing the way we see our no control problems.'

Type of Problem: Can you identify the type your problem is? – *direct control*, *indirect control* or *no control?* When you know this you can see how much control you have over the problem and how much influence you have over the solution.

Write down two of your problems below.
Circle the category each falls into.

Problem 1...
....
....

Direct Control	Indirect Control	No Control
⇩	⇩	⇩
Work on yourself	Influence others by seeking to understand	Change your thinking

Problem 2...
....
....

Direct Control	Indirect Control	No Control
⇩	⇩	⇩
Work on yourself	Influence others by seeking to understand	Change your thinking

Realize Your Response

Generally, problems result when unexpected or unwanted events occur. Therefore it is no surprise that your response to problems is negative.

Responding negatively to problems is a natural reaction, one we all experience. But once you are aware of this negative reaction, you have a choice – to continue with it or seek to change it.

> Your negative reaction to a problem can cause you more pain than the actual problem itself.

Maria's Problem: Maria is frustrated about her son Joseph's messy bedroom. He leaves his clothes, toys and even food on the floor. She yells, '*I have told you to tidy up your room a million times! I'm sick of repeating myself, you are such a lazy slob.*' Joseph replies, '*It's my room, leave me alone, I hate you.*' They engage in a bitter argument.

After the outburst Maria feels worse than she did before. Before she was frustrated; now she is very upset about the words spoken between her and Joseph. Her negative reaction to the problem has created more problems between them. She realizes that she needs to change her response to dealing with problems. She decided to be more proactive.

Instead of yelling at him, Maria decides that she will spell out the consequences if Joseph doesn't listen to her in future. She explains to Joseph that if he disobeys her again she will take away his computer games.

> How am I going to respond? Do I want to be reactive and negative or do I want to be proactive and helpful?

Covey encourages us to use our personal power. He writes,

> *'Look at the word responsibility – "response-ability" – the ability to choose your response.'*

It is essential to realize that with every problem you have the power to choose your response. You choose how you 'act' i.e. reactive or proactive.

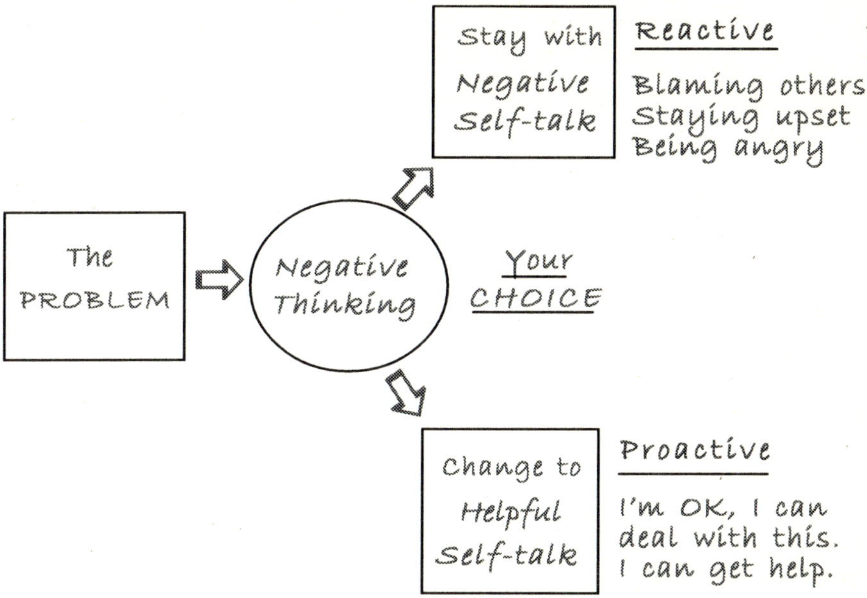

Reactive people:

- Do not take responsibility for their problems and responses, e.g. *She made me angry.*

- Seek to blame other people or circumstances, e.g. *It's his fault.*

- Use excuses to remain stuck in a problem, e.g. *It's just not fair.*

A reactive person becomes a *victim* of their feelings. If they are having a good day they feel happy. If something goes wrong they feel unhappy and blame the problem. The *problem acts on them* so they indulge in negative feelings and seek to escape responsibility.

A reactive person dwells on negative thinking and becomes stuck in the problem.

Proactive people:

- Take responsibility for their problems and responses, e.g. *I can deal with this.*

- Do not blame others or circumstances, e.g. *The solution is in me.*

- Do not make excuses for their problems, e.g. *I may need to seek help.*

A proactive person draws on their *personal power*, not their feelings. They seek to take responsibility for their problems and their actions. They choose to *act on the problem* and work on what they can influence.

A proactive person aims to keep their focus on helpful thinking and finding a solution.

Reactive response

One Saturday morning Liam says to his wife, Hana, 'I'm going to play golf with Matt.' Hana feels upset and unhappy upon hearing this. She reacts angrily, 'I'm sick of you spending all your time with your friends. You never help me around the house or with the kids. You are always upsetting me. You're just a lazy selfish #&*!.' Liam walks out the front door, slamming it shut.

Proactive response

The next Saturday morning Liam tells Hana he is going to play golf with Matt again. Hana feels upset and unhappy, but instead of letting fly she stops to think about what she can say.

'How would you feel if I went out and left you alone with the kids all day?' she asks him. 'In fact, tomorrow I am going out shopping all day with Jen, so you can take care of the kids alone!' Her response makes Liam stop and think.

Re-train Your Brain

In theory this all sounds great and ideally what you want to do is to seek a proactive response to all your problems. Alas, in practice, in the real world, it just isn't that easy.

Do you recall how easy it was when you first tried to drive a car? If you are like most people, training your brain to operate a vehicle was not easy. However, after many lessons and practicing driving, you slowly became more confident and driving a car became less difficult. After months of driving, your brain became adequately trained and driving a car became easy.

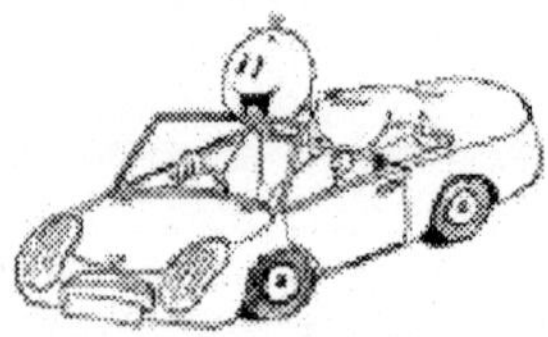

In the same way, by regularly using the four tips you can re-train your brain to choose a proactive response when problems arise. Being reactive and falling victim to negative thoughts is learnt behavior. You can unlearn it.

A proactive response is about challenging negative thinking and replacing it with thoughts which are more rational, realistic and helpful.

STOP NEGATIVE THINKING

When you're feeling upset, anxious, sad, or angry etc, your negative thoughts are creating these feelings.

There are two easy ways to stop negative thoughts from overwhelming you – **thought break** and **jot down**.

1. Thought Break – break negative thought habits by doing something that will distract you.

Instant thought breakers

- count backwards from 100
- read out loud for 5 minutes
- sing your favorite song
- write out a gratitude list
- do a crossword puzzle
- listen to a talking book on CD

When you break your negative thinking, unpleasant feelings will subside and you will be in a better state of mind to focus on solutions.

It's your negative thinking that will keep you down, not the problem.

2. Jot Down – write down or type out your thoughts so you can see what you are really thinking. When you see your negative thoughts you can change them to helpful thoughts.

Slow down your thinking – what are you saying to yourself about the problem? See the words in writing then you will know what thoughts need changing.

For example:

Negative thought: 'Asking other people for help is a sign of weakness'.

START HELPFUL THINKING

Ask yourself, 'what helpful words can I say to myself?' Write these helpful words down. Say them out loud. Repeat saying them three times.

For example:

Helpful thought: 'Seeking help from others leads to solutions. Successful people seek help to find solutions.'

You can not avoid running into problems, but you have total control over your thinking. You can learn to move from negative thoughts onto helpful thoughts. The four simple tips **will help you do this quickly and easily.**

But it's not fair!

Avoid being caught up with the cries of unfairness. You may well be right, it is not fair, you didn't cause the problem. Unfortunately, you still have to deal with all your problems, not just the ones you caused. You need to accept that life is not fair, this is the same for everyone.

The four tips help you turn the fairness table around. Your ability to deal with unfair problems very much depends on your attitude. When life brings on those unfair problems – and it will – use the tips to fight back. When life is not fair, you will have the personal power to be fair to yourself.

By using the four tips you develop a 'can do' attitude.

Norman Vincent Peale, renowned as the 'father of positive thinking', emphasizes how you need to have faith in your ability to deal with problems. In *The Amazing Results of Positive Thinking*, Peale writes:

> 'Belief is one of the most powerful of all problem dissolvers.'

In *Think and Grow Rich*, Napoleon Hill explains that although our subconscious mind is a very powerful asset, most people do not fully utilize its power.

Your subconscious mind works twenty-four hours a day, seven days a week - even while you sleep. During your waking hours, your subconscious will work on your most dominant thinking.

Hill emphasizes how your subconscious works on what you desire the most through your emotions, feelings and senses. He writes:

> 'Your subconscious mind recognizes and acts upon ONLY thoughts which have been well-mixed with emotion or feeling.'

When dealing with any problem, the greater your desire to focus on a solution, the more this desire will enter your subconscious mind. And in turn, your subconscious will help you in your efforts to find a solution.

The four tips help your mind focus on solutions and thus tap into the power of your subconscious.

Applying the four tips enables you to re-train your brain towards helpful thinking. Each tip has its own unique role in helping you focus on solutions. The next four chapters reveal the power of these tips.

1. **Define - define the problem**

   This tip helps you to 'see it as it is – not worse than it is'. You will stop being a victim of negative thinking. When you see and understand what is really going on, the solution is closer at hand.

2. **Own - own the problem**

   This tip is the 'power tip' - it is about taking control. When you own the problem you can take control of the problem. With control you have the power to find solutions.

3. **Truth - face the truth**

   This is the crucial tip that asks you to 'check that your thinking is helpful and true'. Without the truth the right solution will not be realized.

4. **Balance - keep the balance**

   This tip reminds you to 'keep the end in mind'. You are on a 'life journey'. Your life journey will end one day, you need to keep problems in perspective.

THAT'S SMART THINKING FOR A STREET BUM.
SUPPORT THE FIGHT AGAINST NEGATIVE INCOME
A STREET BUM NEEDS TO KEEP UP WITH THE FINANCIAL TIMES.
SUPPORT THE FIGHT AGAINST NEGATIVE INCOME
JEFF LANG

CHAPTER 4

Define Tip

See it as it is, not
worse than it is.

TIP 1

Define the problem

by

seeking to understand

The **define tip** asks you to examine and understand the problem. Problems put you in a negative state of mind, so it's important to 'see it as it is – not worse than it is'. Seeing the real problem leads to solutions.

Are you being a good doctor to your problems? How would you feel about a doctor who didn't take the time to examine you or ask you questions when you are sick? Would you trust their prescription?

In the same way a doctor seeks to diagnose an illness correctly and then discern the correct treatment, you need to examine your problem and then discern the correct solution.

In *The 7 Habits of Highly Effective People,* Covey stresses the importance of first 'diagnosing the problem' correctly before seeking to 'prescribe a solution'.

The following strategies help you to define the problem correctly.

- Understand the problem
- Realize your thoughts
- Seek calm and quiet
- Express your emotions
- Write to heal

Understand the problem

Your strategy: *examine the problem*

1. **Type of problem**

What type is your problem? - Is it direct, indirect or no control? See pages 22-25.

For example: An Indirect Problem

Sulyn and Gina are flat mates. Mostly they get on well, but one night they start arguing over an orange. Hayden, a friend, walks into the kitchen. 'What's with all the yelling?' he asks. 'What's the problem?'

'I bought this orange but Gina says it's hers,' Sulyn explains, 'she says that she bought it.' Gina interrupts. 'I did bu;y it and I want it!'

Hayden rolls his eyes. 'Why don't you just share it?' 'I need the whole orange,' replies Gina. 'And I need the whole orange,' Sulyn retorts.

'Well then,' Hayden admits, 'we really do have a problem.' He decides to examine the problem more closely. 'Why do you want the orange, Sulyn?' Sulyn answers, 'I need the peel for a cake.' Hayden turns to Gina. 'And why do you want it?' 'I need the juice for my smoothie,' she replies. 'There you go, Gina can juice the orange and then give it to Sulyn for the peel.'

2. Topics and Issues

Often problems are expressed as topics when the real issue is not recognized. Until the real issue (that is the underlying cause) is identified, finding a solution is an endless struggle.

Topic – the surface appearance of the problem

Issue – the underlying cause of the problem

Common Topics	**Real Issue**
Spending	Control
Lies	Trust
Neglect	Love
Jealousy	Insecurity
Abuse	Power
Misbehavior	Discipline

What is the number one topic couples argue about?
Answer: **money**

What is the real issue?
Answer: **control**

You can't solve money problems with more money – why?

Answer: **Because it is about control.**

If you can't control your money (i.e. your spending) on a $50,000 income, you will not be able to control your spending on a $1,000,000 income.

Realize your thoughts

Your strategy: *check your thoughts*

When problems arise you automatically assume that it is the problem that is making you feel upset and unhappy.

You need to realize that your negative thoughts are making you feel upset and unhappy, not the problem.

Given that most of our thoughts are automatic, you often don't realize what your negative thoughts are. Unless you make the effort to check your thinking.

Negative thoughts come first, this produces negative feelings. If you change your thoughts, your feelings will change.

When you are feeling upset, ask yourself – what am I thinking?

Once you realize what your negative thoughts are, you can try to look for helpful thoughts.

You can not always control problems, but you always have control of your thoughts.

Seek calm and quiet

Your strategy: *think calmly and clearly*

It is essential that you stay calm when dealing with problems. In *The Amazing Results of Positive Thinking,* Peale writes:

> 'When a difficulty arises, the first tendency is to become upset, even panicky. Nervously we assume that the problem has to be solved right away, quick; that something must be done immediately.'

Negative thinking is the reason why many people feel stressed by problems. Use thought breakers to stop negative thoughts from overwhelming you – see pg 33.

Staying calm is critical as your brain cannot function properly under distress. When your mind is calm and quiet you turn 'melodrama' into a 'mellow-drama'. Peale also writes:

> 'So I must stress the importance of learning the use of silence in meeting life's difficult problems.'

To achieve the best results in thinking about a problem, find a quiet and private place. Take long deep breaths if you need to calm yourself down.

Express your emotions

Your strategy: *release your emotions*

Talking about problems is the best way to give your feelings a voice and release pent-up emotions. Pent-up emotions make it very difficult to keep your mind relaxed and open to possible solutions.

If you don't want to talk about your problems with someone else or if you have no one you can talk to, then take the time to talk to yourself. Write down or type out how you feel or just speak out aloud to yourself. You need to give your feelings a voice to release any pain.

The act of putting pen to paper also provides you with a physical outlet for emotions. Writing can empower you to fight off feelings of helplessness. The written word also reveals your state of mind and shows if you need to seek help.

Talking to someone, writing down or typing your thoughts can help you begin the healing process of overcoming painful problems and to see your way to solutions.

Write to heal

Your strategy: *experience healing power*

The simple act of putting pen to paper, of writing, can help you to heal. Dr James Pennebaker, scientist and professor of psychology in the USA, has undertaken extensive research on the power of writing.

His studies on the effects of writing on health have been widely accepted around the world. Dr Pennebaker reveals how writing is not only good for your emotional wellbeing, but also good for your physical health.

In his book, *Writing to Heal*, Dr Pennebaker explains how writing not only helps, but how it can also heal. Taking the time to write about problems and expressing emotions can have a positive effect on the immune system.

His studies indicate that the release writing offers has a direct effect on the body's ability to withstand stress and to fight off illness. If your emotions are not expressed or released this can lead to mental and physical illness such as depression and stress.

In writing you give your feelings a voice. Expressing your feelings in written words can also change the way you think about and see problems.

Define the Problem

Assess your problem

Complete the checklist below to see if you have defined your problem correctly. Circle 'yes' or 'no'.

1.	Do you know what type the problem is and where your influence lies?	Yes	No
2.	Can you see how your negative thoughts are making you feel unhappy, not the problem itself?	Yes	No
3.	Do you have a quiet, private place to think about the problem?	Yes	No
4.	Are you willing to express all your emotions and release any negative thoughts that are upsetting you?	Yes	No
5.	Have you identified the real issue, and stopped arguing about topics?	Yes	No

If you have answered 'no' to any of the above questions, you need to work towards a 'yes' if you want to solve your problem.

Using the **Problem Solving Guide** in Part 2 will help you to define your problem correctly.

One evening an elderly couple are sitting in their lounge room watching TV. The wife turns to her husband during an ad break and says, 'I would really love some ice-cream.'

'Okay,' he says. 'I'll get it for you.' 'Well,' says the wife, 'you had better write it down.'

'No,' her husband replies. 'Don't be silly, I can remember something that simple.'

'I also want chocolate topping,' the wife adds, 'so you had better write it down.' 'I don't need to,' he insists.

Half an hour later the husband returns from the kitchen, holding a plate of bacon and fried eggs. 'Here you are,' he says.

His wife looks at him, shaking her head. 'I told you to write it down!' she retorts. 'I wanted the eggs poached, not fried!'

IT SAYS HERE THAT ONE CHOCOLATE BAR HAS THE SAME CALORIES AS 30 CELERY STICKS.
I'LL TAKE THE CHOCOLATE BAR, THANK-YOU.
JEFF LANG

CHAPTER 5

Own Tip

Take control and
feel the power.

TIP 2

Own the problem

by

taking responsibility

The **own tip** gives you power. When you own the problem and take 100% responsibility for it, you will have 100% power to find a solution.

> You create what does or doesn't happen to you, by what you do or what you don't do.

Most of us have been conditioned to blame someone or something else for our problems. Most people do not understand what it really means to take 100% responsibility.

In her best-seller, *Feel the Fear and Do It Anyway*, Susan Jeffers explains that 'Taking responsibility means never blaming anyone else for anything you are being, doing, having or feeling.'

Taking 100% responsibility means:

- Stop blaming others
- Stop blaming yourself
- Stop making excuses
- Fight criticism and defeat
- Face the pain

Stop blaming others

Give up blaming others or circumstances. Don't act like a victim.

Avoid playing the *blame game*. Blaming others for your problems only makes you a victim.

When it comes to problems you need to accept the reality of life – *life is not fair*. Whether the problem is your fault or not isn't the issue. If a problem affects you, then it's your problem. Blaming does not lead to solutions.

In *Life Strategies*, Dr Phil writes:

'When you set out to find the causes of your problems in other people, you'll never find them, because they aren't there. They're in you.'

By blaming someone else you give up your personal power and control of your life. The solution always lies within you, not someone else.

Stop blaming yourself

Avoid blaming yourself. Don't make yourself a victim.

Blaming yourself for a problem will also make you a victim and this only causes more problems. By putting yourself down you are working against yourself.

> '*If only* I had listened ...': such statements keep you stuck in the past. Let go of the past.

> '*What if* I fail?': such statements keep you in fear of the future. Focus on thoughts of success.

In his book *How to Stop Worrying and Start Living*, Dale Carnegie stresses the importance of living for today. You need to let go the regrets of the past and the anxiety for the future.

> You cannot change what you did before, but you can change what you are doing now.

Always be your own best friend and say to yourself:

I am okay. I did the best I could with what I knew. I will seek to know more, so I can do better in the future.

Stop making excuses

Be aware of when you are making excuses.

In *Feel the Fear and Do It Anyway*, Jeffers explains how the *victim mentality* can be very subtle and often takes on many unrecognized forms. When you make excuses for not dealing with problems, you are acting like a victim.

I want to lose weight but I don't have time to exercise.

I want to get out of debt but I don't know how to.

I can't stop myself when I want to buy something.

I know I should give up smoking, but it's too hard.

If you can relate to any of the above, then you have put yourself in the *excuses trap*. You need to stop making excuses and start taking action. Getting help when you are stuck is the best course of action.

Fight criticism and defeat

Protect yourself against self-criticism and self-defeat.

You need to stay mentally strong when dealing with problems. When problems arise there will always be those who seek someone to blame. It may well be you who is the blame target.

> Avoid letting others' criticism of you turn into self-criticism.
>
> Avoid letting others' rejection of you turn into self-defeat.

The strongest words you hear are in your head – *your self-talk.* Words are very powerful. You need to watch what you say to yourself. Your self-talk can work for you or against you.

> Say 'NO' to negative self-talk.
> Say 'YES' to helpful self-talk.

In *The Amazing Results of Positive Thinking,* Peale explains how people often practice self-defeat and tell themselves they can't deal with the problem. If you think thoughts of defeat, you will be defeated. Keep your focus on helpful thinking.

Face the pain

Accept there may be some pain as you work towards a solution.

The hardest aspect of problems is dealing with the pain. Nobody likes going through pain, so it is only natural to fear pain.

In *Feel the Fear and Do It Anyway*, Jeffers reveals how the 'fear of pain' is often worse than 'going through the pain'.

Being stuck in the fear of pain is worse than going through the pain.

- When you go through pain, the problem can be resolved and the pain disappears.
- When you live in the fear of pain, the problem remains and so does the pain.
- Don't be afraid of being uncomfortable. Don't be so afraid of going through some pain. You don't have to do it alone – seek help.

Yvonne's Problem: 'I can't go through with it,' said my fiance, Josh. I will never forget how those words hit me – like a black wave had engulfed me, I couldn't breathe.

Just one week before our wedding. How could he do this to me? Despite my pleading and yelling, he gave no explanation. He just left. The next day I started running, I ran and ran and ran until I was physically exhausted. While running I kept repeating my mantra – this pain is only temporary, this pain is only temporary. With tears streaming down my face, I just kept running and repeating my mantra.

For two weeks I ran before work, and then after work, repeating my mantra. With each day the pain slowly subsided. Until the worst was over and the black wave was gone, I could breathe again. I stopped blaming Josh for my pain and accepted that he wasn't the right person for me.

Focus all your efforts on what you can do and don't get caught up on what you can't do. When you understand that you have control over your thinking, you can move from the feeling of pain to a feeling of power.

Even if the only thing you can do is change your thinking, you can work on that.

Own the Problem

Assess your problem

Complete the checklist below to see if you are taking responsibility for your problems. Circle 'yes' or 'no'.

1. Are you blaming someone else for your problem? Yes No

2. Are you blaming yourself for your problem? Yes No

3. Are you making excuses for the problem? Yes No

4. Are you giving in to self-criticism and self-defeat? Yes No

5. Are you avoiding the pain of the problem? Yes No

If you answered 'yes' to any of the above questions, you are not taking responsibility for your problems.

You need to work towards 'no' to get your personal power back. Using the **Problem Solving Guide** in Part 2 will help you.

When everybody on earth was dead and waiting to enter Paradise, God appeared and said, 'I want the men to make two lines. One line for the men who were true heads of their household and the other line for the men who were dominated by their wives. I want all the women to report to St Peter.'

Soon the women were gone, and there were two lines of men. The line of the men who were dominated by their wives was 100 miles long, and in the line of men who truly were heads of their household there was only one man.

God said, 'You men should be ashamed of yourselves. I created you to be the heads of your households. You have been disobedient and have not fulfilled your purpose! Of all of you, only one obeyed. Learn from him.'

God turned to the one man, 'How did you manage to be the only one?' The man replied, 'My wife told me to stand here.'

I NEED HELP
WHATS THE PROBLEM.
LIBRARY
INFO i
I HATE IT WHEN PEOPLE USE BIG WORDS I DON'T UNDERSTAND.
YES THE VERBOSITY IN LINGUISTICS CAN BE BOTH PERPLEXING AND IRRITATING.
LIBRARY
JEFF LANG

CHAPTER 6

Truth Tip

Face the truth to
see solutions.

TIP 3

Face the truth

with

helpful thinking

Of the four tips, the **truth tip** is the most challenging of all, the one that says:

You cannot solve problems if
you don't face the truth.

In *Life Strategies*, Dr Phil explains that facing the truth is more than just about saying,

- yes, I have a problem.

Facing the truth is about asking yourself:

- what am I doing?
- what am I believing?
- what am I not doing?
- what am I putting up with?

... that has caused this problem.

Dr Phil's truth motto is: ***You can't change what you don't acknowledge.***

One truth that you must face – no excuses, no buts, no denials – is that you play a role in all your problems.

You are part of the problem.

This is actually good news, because it means:

You are part of the solution.

Check the Truth questions – are you facing the truth about your problem? Which question applies to you?

1. ***What am I thinking* that is contributing to the problem?** Have I checked that my thoughts are true? Am I holding onto false thoughts?

2. ***What am I doing* that is contributing to this problem?** Are my actions making the problem worse? What actions can I take to make things better?

3. ***What am I allowing* that is contributing to the problem?** How am I letting others treat me? How am I treating myself?

4. ***What am I saying* that is contributing to the problem?** Am I being part of the solution or am I remaining part of the problem?

5. ***What am I being* that is contributing to the problem?** Am I being a victim? What can I do to help myself deal with the pain?

6. ***What am I not doing* that is contributing to the problem?** Do I need to ask for help? Who can I ask for help? Am I looking for information to learn more about my problem?

Check your beliefs

Are my thoughts true?

The truth tip is about checking your *beliefs*. Your *beliefs* are fixed thoughts you have accepted.

Where your thoughts are in fact true, you form *true beliefs*. But where your thoughts are in fact false, you form *false beliefs*.

Your thoughts can be so ingrained that you seldom question their accuracy and you may not even be aware of them.

> Don't believe everything you think.
>
> Your thoughts are not always true.

Old false thoughts from years ago may still be repeating in your mind and have become a false belief.

Given most of our thoughts are automatic, you do not always pay close attention to what you think.

> You need to ask yourself:
> What am I thinking?
> Are my thoughts true?

You cannot control the negative thoughts that pop into your head. But you can control what you choose to believe.

When you are feeling bad you need to stop and check your thoughts, then you can challenge and change any false thoughts.

Rita's Problem: For years a negative voice in my head kept saying, *You're just not good enough.* I especially disliked the way I looked. I was self-conscious about my body. I felt fat and ugly. I had struggled with my weight for many years, going from one diet to another, trying to get to a wishful number. But, I couldn't stick to any diet.

I looked at my therapist and asked him what he thought of my looks. My therapist asked me, 'has anyone called you ugly?' *Well no*, I answered. Has your doctor said you are overweight, it's dangerous for your health and you need to be a specific number. *Well no*, I repeated.

'So you've made up these false thoughts and you have chosen to believe them,' he continued. 'Not all your thoughts are true. You need to identify the false ones and let them go,' he explained to me.

I came to see what he was saying. I worked on changing my false thoughts to helpful thoughts - *I am ok, I look fine. I will focus on healthy foods, not fad diets.*

Challenging false thoughts means being aware of your automatic negative thoughts and taking a closer look at them.

Louise L. Hay, author of *You Can Heal Your Life* explains, you need to challenge negative thinking and replace it with helpful thinking. She writes, 'Whatever the problem is, it comes from a thought pattern, and thought patterns can be changed!'

I have survived other problems in the past. I will survive this one too.

This problem sucks, but it is only temporary, it won't last forever. I can still enjoy my life.

I'm strong enough to handle this problem. I can accept uncomfortable feelings. Feelings change, no feeling lasts forever.

Using the **Problem Solving Guide** in Part 2 will help you identify your false thoughts and guide you onto helpful thoughts.

Read about the most common false thinking traps on the next two pages so you can be aware of which trap you fall victim to when dealing with problems.

False Thinking Traps

Ten common types of false thinking that make coping with problems more difficult:

1. **Black and white thinking** is seeing life in extremes with no middle ground. For example, *all or nothing, good or bad*, *right or wrong*, *failure or success*. Such value judgments are opinions, not facts. Life is seldom black and white; there are many shades of grey.

2. **Unrealistic expectations** means living with fixed rules and expectations. For example, *I have to*, he *should*, she *must.* When you impose rules or expectations on yourself or others, you feel upset when you or other people do not live up to these expectations.

3. **Selective thinking** is seeing only the negative side of a situation or seeing only your point of view. For example, looking at what is going wrong in your life and ignoring the things that are going right.

4. **Overgeneralizing** is making a big issue out of an isolated event, such as using terms like *always*, *never*, *everyone*, *everything*. For example, *everyone will think I am a failure*, *he never helps me* or *I am always stuffing things up*. It is also using labels to describe others or yourself such as *I am hopeless*, *she is stupid*, *you are so lazy* or *you're an idiot.*

5. **Exaggerating** is making mountains out of mole hills. You focus on the problems so much your feelings become overwhelming; for example, *I'll never meet anyone, I'll always be unhappy*. You feel even more upset.

6. **Catastrophizing** is the tendency to exaggerate negative events in life such as believing a situation to be *terrible*, *awful* or *horrible* when in reality it is only annoying or unpleasant. For example *it's awful being single, it's terrible to make mistakes, it's horrible to be criticized.*

7. **Personalizing** is feeling responsible for other people's problems or actions toward you. For example, *my spouse is unhappy, it's my fault; she didn't enjoy herself, I should have done something.*

8. **Jumping to conclusions** (or fortune-telling) is assuming the worst when things go wrong or seeing other people's comments and actions in a negative way. For example, *my friend didn't ring, she must be upset with me; I am going to fail.*

9. **Mistaking feelings for facts** is confusing feelings with reality, 'I feel therefore I am' thinking. For example, you may believe that because you feel hopeless you are hopeless. Your feelings change over time.

10. **Thinking life should be fair** means believing the world should be a fair place and that you should always be treated fairly. The reality is that life is not fair, because people are not perfect.

To change your false beliefs you need to identify and challenge your false thoughts. Look carefully, can you see your own false thoughts in the examples below?

False Thoughts	**Helpful Thoughts**
I will never get over this.	This pain is temporary. I will get over this and I will be happy again.
My life is a mess, I hate living.	There are good and bad times in everyone's life. I will be grateful for what I have. I will seek to improve myself.
I'm so disappointed in myself, I am such a failure.	Everyone wins and fails in life. The winners are the ones who keep trying.
I've let people down, they hate me now.	I made some mistakes, we all make mistakes. Not everyone has to like me. I still like me.
There is nothing I can do, I can't change what happened.	I can't change the past but I can change what I choose to do now.
My partner is getting me down.	My negative thinking is getting me down. I can change my thinking.
No one can help me, it's too late now.	As long as I am willing to keep looking for help, I will find it.

False Thoughts	**Helpful Thoughts**
I must have the approval of others.	I won't worry about what other people may think, this is my life.
I must be careful not to make mistakes.	Everyone makes mistakes no matter how careful they are, it is part of life.
It is terrible when things go wrong.	People are not perfect and life is not perfect. Accept that things go wrong in life.
It is easier to avoid problems than to face them.	Avoiding problems leads to more problems, that makes life even harder.
I have no control over how I feel when things go wrong.	My thinking about things that go wrong determines how I feel. I can change my thinking and so my feelings will change.
My relationship was perfect before this problem happened.	No relationship is ever perfect. I am idealizing the past.
I need to be loved and in a relationship to be happy.	I need to love myself. It's okay to be single, I can still enjoy life.
I keep struggling with money problems. I am always living in debt.	I need a money plan, to take control of my spending or to get help.

Check your perception

How am I seeing my problem?

The truth tip is also about checking your *perception*. Your *perception* is the way that you see things. In *Life Strategies*, 'Dr Phil' writes, 'You have the power to choose your perceptions.'

A problem is only as bad as your thinking will allow. When dealing with a problem – ask yourself: 'how am I seeing this problem?'

> You don't react to an event.
> You react to your thinking
> (perception) about the event.

Is your perception of the problem based on 'true and current facts' or is it based on 'false beliefs and bad past experiences'?

True and current facts means seeing the problem as just a setback. You will feel that you can deal with it. You may need more information or even some help.

False beliefs and bad past experiences means seeing the problem as a disaster. You believe you can not deal with it and think that things always go wrong for you.

Successful people choose to see their problems as a temporary setback. They strive to create *value from adversity*.

Anthony's Problem: In his best-selling book *Awaken the Giant Within*, Anthony Robbins recalls one of the most devastating problems in his life. He discovered that his company was $758,000 in debt due to the mismanagement of his money by one of his business partners.

Robbins was advised by experts to give up and declare bankruptcy. But his perception of the problem was very different. He took full responsibility for not keeping an eye on his finances and set out to overcome the problem. His perception was true and based on current facts.

For Robbins it was a chance to prove himself. He committed to creating *value from adversity* and worked harder than he ever had before. His efforts took his company to a new level of success and he became a household name. He is considered one of the best known 'life coaches' in the US. Robbins writes about his life challenges:

'It's not the events that shape my life that determine how I feel and act, but, rather, it's the way I *interpret* and *evaluate* my life experiences.'

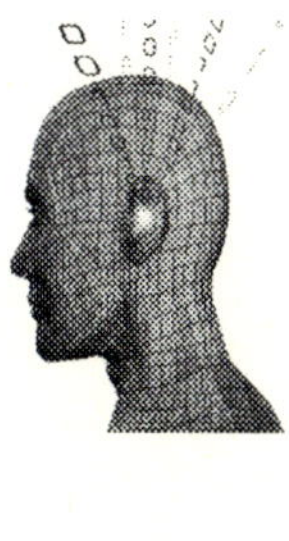

Changing false perceptions

Past events affect me

Are you living in the past?

You cannot change your past but you can change how you think now – you can stop living in the past.

If you continue to see life through false perceptions created by bad past events, you are letting your past control you.

For example, if you see yourself as 'always failing' because you failed in the past, you need to test this. Have you ever succeeded in anything?

Yes, you sometimes succeed and you sometimes fail. Saying 'you always fail' is false. The truth is everyone fails and succeeds. In fact successful people fail the most, because they keep trying until they succeed. They 'fail forward' to success.

> You may not have been responsible for what happened to you in the past, but you are responsible for how you act now.

Check that your perception of a problem is based on true and current facts, not on false beliefs and bad past experiences.

My reaction is caused by others

Do you believe you are controlled by other people's words?

For example, 'he made me so angry, that is why I threw the mug at him'. While what someone says will affect you, the decision to act on it is your choice.

Once you are aware of your reaction – such as 'anger' – you have a choice: you can act out your anger or you can walk away. Other people cannot control your response, only you can.

> You may not be responsible for an upsetting event, but you are responsible for how you respond to it – how you think and act.

No matter what someone says to you, it is your choice as to whether you accept their words. Your reaction comes from your thoughts, not from other people's words.

> You cannot turn off your feelings, but you can turn off your behavior.

Life circumstances control me

Do you believe you are controlled by life events?

For example, 'I am miserable and bitter because I lost my job'. Life events do not control you. It is your thoughts that control you.

Losing your job (the event) is not the cause of you being unhappy. Rather, your negative thoughts (self-talk) about losing your job are causing you to be unhappy.

1. The event: *losing your job*
2. Your self-talk: *unhappy thoughts*
3. Your reaction: *unhappy feelings*

It is important to note (1) does not cause (3). It is always the case that (2) causes (3).

It is natural to feel negative when things go wrong, but once you recognize these negative feelings you can choose to continue with negative thoughts or seek to change to helpful thoughts.

No matter what the problem, you always have personal power. You have the power to change your thinking, to change your reaction and to seek help.

I can not change

Do you believe that you can not change?

For example, 'I can't change, it's too late for me'.

Your life choices so far have made you who you are today. You can continue with those same choices or you can seek to make different life choices.

You can choose how you want to be and you can change when you need to. You always have the personal power to change your thinking.

> If you start making different choices your life will change. If you seek to change your false beliefs you will change.

If you are unhappy with your life, what are you thinking that is stopping you from changing and getting the life you want?

Do you think you will fail? Are you afraid of failing? Do you see failure as bad? Failure is not bad. You cannot succeed if you do not risk failure.

All successful people see failure as okay, it brings them closer to success. Not trying is what really limits your potential.

False Perception	**True Perception**
She made me angry, that is why I hit her.	I chose to react with anger. I could have walked away.
I am this way because I was verbally abused as a child.	I am this way because I keep repeating the words of abuse to myself today.
I am overweight and I can't help overeating.	I eat for emotional comfort. I could seek emotional comfort some other way.
I get upset when other people criticize me.	I cannot change what other people say, but I don't have to accept their words.
I am stressed at work; there's too much to do.	I will do only what I can and keep a better perspective. It is only a job, not my life.
If I leave my abusive boyfriend, I will be single and may never meet anyone else.	It is better to be healthy and single than be abused in a sick relationship. I need to love myself first to find real love.

Using the **Problem Solving Guide** in Part 2 will help you check that your perception is true and guide you onto helpful thinking.

Ask Better Questions

To solve problems you need to ask good questions. When faced with a problem do you demand answers to the 'blame' question or 'why me' question?

Who caused this problem? Why is this happening to me? These are *reactive* and *negative* questions. If you ask such questions, you will not move toward solutions.

When it comes to solving problems, good questions lead you to better answers. By learning how to ask *proactive* and *helpful* questions you help yourself and others as well. Ask better questions and you will get better answers.

In *Awaken the Giant Within,* Robbins comments on how asking good questions helped him get through the most difficult problems in his life. He writes:

> **'Learning to ask empowering questions in moments of crisis is a critical skill** that has pulled me through some of the toughest times in my life.'

Negative Questions

Avoid asking reactive questions that keep you stuck in the problem.

- Whose fault is this problem?
- Why is this happening to me?
- Why is life so unfair?
- Why am I such a failure?

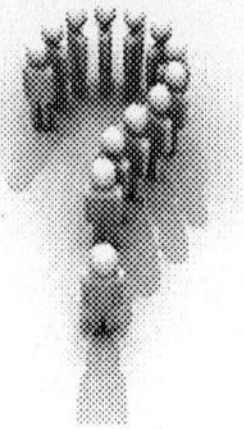

Helpful Questions

Ask proactive questions that keep you focused on finding a solution.

- What can I learn from this problem?
- What is good about this problem?
- How can I change my thinking?
- Who can I ask for help?
- Where can I find helpful information?
- What is the funny side of this?

The best helpful questions you can ask yourself are: *how can I learn from this problem?* and *what is good about this problem?* These questions will make you feel better about yourself and your life.

The Problem Solving Guide in Part 2 of this book gives you helpful questions that will lead you toward solutions.

George and Quan's Problem: Both George and Quan have lost their jobs in the IT industry due to a downturn in the economy.

George asked himself: *why is life so unfair?, why is this happening to me?, why am I such a loser?, how am I going to find another job during a recession?, how am I going to cope?* These negative questions kept George stuck in his problem. It took him a long time to find another job.

Quan asked himself: *where can I find a job agency?, who can I talk to about getting a good reference?, which companies can I visit and leave my resume?, how would I like to move forward in my career?* These helpful questions led Quan to the right job opportunity and he got a job at a better position than his last job.

In *Awaken the Giant Within,* Robbins comments on how asking helpful questions is one of the secrets to success. He writes:

> 'I realized that the main difference between the people who seemed to be successful – in any area! – and those who weren't was that **successful people asked better questions, and as a result, they got better answers.**'

Face the Truth

Assess your problem

Complete the checklist below to see if you are facing the truth about your problem. Circle 'yes' or 'no'.

1. Are you willing to admit the truth about the problem? Yes No

2. Can you see the role you play in the problem? Yes No

3. Is there something that you are doing or not doing, or putting up with, that caused this problem? Yes No

4. Have you checked your beliefs are true? Yes No

5. Have you checked your perception is based on true and current facts? Yes No

6. Are you willing to admit that you may need help and seek it? Yes No

If you answered 'no' to any of the above questions, you are not facing the truth. You need to work towards 'yes' if you want to find solutions. Using the Problem Solving Guide in Part 2 will help you.

A woman takes her husband to the doctor. After examining him the doctor asks to speak to his wife alone. He explains, 'Your husband is suffering from a very severe level of stress. If you don't do the following, your husband will die; it is just a matter of time.'

The doctor says to the wife, 'You must do the following: Always be pleasant and kind to him. For breakfast, lunch and dinner prepare only meals you know he loves. Don't burden him with chores. Don't discuss your problems with him, it will only increase his stress level and hasten his demise. Most importantly, you will need to make love with your husband every night and satisfy his every whim. If you can do this for the next year he will regain his health.'

As the wife was driving her husband home, he asked her, 'What did the doctor say to you?' The wife replied, 'You're going to die.'

WOO HOO!
HOORAY!
YEAH!
WOO HOO!
HOORAY!
THE ROCKING STONES
BOO, GO HOME!
ROCKING STONES MANAGER
ROCK BAND BOOED
JEFF LANG

CHAPTER 7

Balance Tip

Check the bigger picture.

TIP 4

Keep the balance

by

using perspective

The **balance tip** reminds you to keep your thinking in perspective with your life journey.

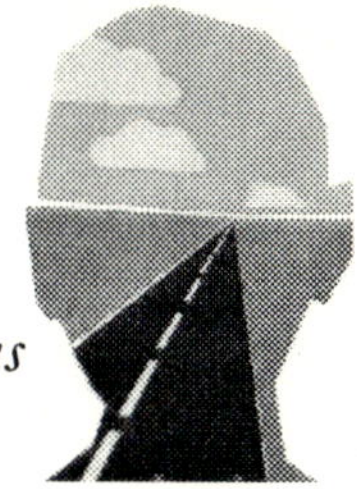

Your life journey had a beginning and it will have an end.
Ask yourself: *Am I letting my problems spoil my life journey?*

If you become stuck on a problem and live in a problem, you will lose perspective and your life will be out of balance.

Problems are a part of life.
You need to live with problems,
not live *in* problems.

The key to keeping your problems in perspective is to have a strong and stable sense of who you are and what your values are.

By knowing who you are and what your values are, you form your *personal laws*.

Your *personal laws* are your compass that guides you on the best path to take on your life journey. Your *personal laws* help you navigate through the potholes in life called 'problems'.

The laws of society seek to protect you from harm, ensure your rights are respected, and help you when laws are broken. As with the laws of society, your personal laws should protect you, respect you and serve you. For an example of *Personal Laws* see below.

My Personal Laws

To protect, to respect and to serve me

Take care of my body with a good diet, regular exercise and enough sleep.

Take care of my mind. Pay attention to my thoughts and feelings.

Spend quality time with family & friends.

Always love myself first. Respect and love others. Expect respect from others.

Spend less than I earn. Meet my needs first and then my wants only if I can afford to.

Be forgiving to others and to myself, because no one is perfect.

Find my passion and pursue my dreams. Develop my own talents and interests.

Always remember this is my life journey and it will end one day.

My Personal Laws

To protect, to respect and to serve me

(Write down your own personal laws)

Your Center

Do you know what is at the center of your life?

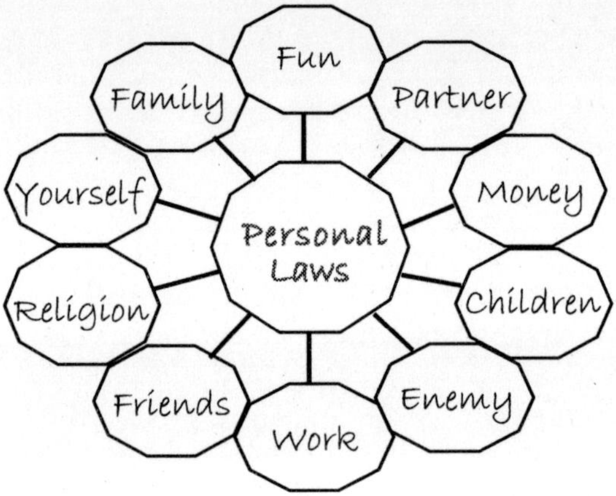

In *The 7 Habits of Highly Effective People*, Covey explains how we all have a center in our life. To live a balanced life you need your personal laws at the center of your life.

By having personal laws at your center you know that no matter what happens in other areas of life, your center will remain stable and in your control.

In contrast, if you are people-centered or object-centered, your center can change any moment without warning, because you are being controlled by that person or object.

Being partner-centered

If your partner or spouse is the center of your life what will happen to you if your partner leaves or dies? You will lose your center. When you have problems with your partner, again your center will be affected and will become unstable.

Being children-centered

If your children are the center of your life, when they grow up and leave, you will lose your center. If you are constantly struggling and fighting with them, your center will be unstable.

Being work-centered

If you live for your job and develop your identity from that job, your center is vulnerable to change. If you lose your job you will lose your center and your sense of identity.

Being wealth-centered

If you are money driven and gain your self-worth by your income and possessions, you will be vulnerable to anything that affects your wealth. If you lose your wealth you will be living with an unstable center.

Being self-centered

If you are self-centered, then you are focused more on taking than giving. Your center is constantly changing and unstable as you continue to live by your changing wants and fickle feelings.

Being personal laws-centered

Your personal laws will not divorce you, be destroyed by fire, get angry at you, or change unexpectedly. Your personal laws are your stable foundation and will remain so. If you decide to change any of your personal laws, it will be a change that you control and that only you can make.

Being people- or object-centered makes you very vulnerable to problems with that person or object which you can not control.

You need a stable and unchanging center. While other areas of your life are subject to change at any moment, your (center) personal laws remain constant and unchanging. Unless, of course, you decide to make a change.

When your center is your personal laws, you deal with problems by stepping back from the emotions of a problem.

You keep a balanced view by looking at your family needs, work needs, money needs and any other needs that are involved with the problem.

You search for a solution that takes all the needs into consideration. You are not driven by other people, emotions or circumstances. You are driven by your own personal laws.

Deepak's Problem: I phoned my wife Aliyah, it was Friday afternoon. Honey, the boss asked me to work this weekend. She replied, 'I hope you said no. We organized the trip to the beach. You promised the kids.'

Can't we go next weekend? 'It's always next weekend, you have been saying next weekend for months now,' she exclaimed. Think about the extra money, we could use it. She replied, 'the kids don't want money, they want to see their dad.' But honey, come on, we can go next week, what's the rush?

'What's the rush you ask?', she repeats angrily, 'as if your family isn't important. Think about this question: How many people on their death bed, express regret and wish they had spent more time at work?' She was right, I was letting work overtake my life. Spending time with my kids was important to me. I told my boss, sorry, can't work this weekend. I have a family event to attend.

A person centered on their personal laws:

- sees problems differently
- thinks about problems differently
- reacts to problems differently

They are driven by their own personal laws, not by their emotions.

Your Reaction

Emotion driven people become victims to negative thoughts and let them continue as unhelpful thinking. This produces negative results in their life.

Mariel's Problem: Mariel and her husband Rico don't talk anymore. He is always busy with work, and working on his car. She feels lonely and neglected in the marriage and has started having thoughts of divorce. Rico just doesn't make her smile and happy anymore. She thinks it's Rico's fault that she is so unhappy and their marriage is failing.

Personal laws driven people seek to challenge negative thoughts and engage in helpful thinking. This gives positive results in their life.

Brie's Problem Brie and her partner Xavier don't seem to spend much time together anymore. He is always busy with work. When he comes home he checks out in front of the TV. Brie feels lonely and neglected.
After some self-reflection she decides to create the life she wants, instead of waiting on Xavier all the time. She realizes it only takes one person to make change happen. She works on what she can do. She asks Xavier out to see a film with her or she will go with a friend. As she makes the effort to change, Xavier begins to respond and in turn makes an effort to change himself.

Your Perspective

Don't Sweat the Small Stuff has a very simple message and its author Richard Carlson delivers it with great insight. Keep your problems in perspective with your life journey. Carlson writes:

> **'Ask yourself the question – will this matter a year from now?'**

If the answer is 'no', don't waste your time being upset about it today. Learn to let the small stuff go. But, what if the answer is 'yes'?

In *What About the Big Stuff?* Carlson explains that you also need to keep difficult problems in perspective. He writes:

> **'The big stuff also teaches (or reminds) us of life's short duration and preciousness.'**

One thought that forces you to see problems in perspective is your mortality – your life has an expiry date. Focus on what you can do and decide to continue enjoying your life journey.

Your Decision

In *Feel the Fear and Do it Anyway,* Jeffers explains how it can be difficult to make a decision. You may be afraid of making the wrong decision. This fear can stop you from moving forward in life.

Do not simply look at a decision as being either right or wrong. Instead look at decisions as different life paths you can follow.

If you choose one decision you take path A, if you choose another decision you take path B. Whichever path you choose you make the best choice with what you know and most importantly you are dealing with the problem.

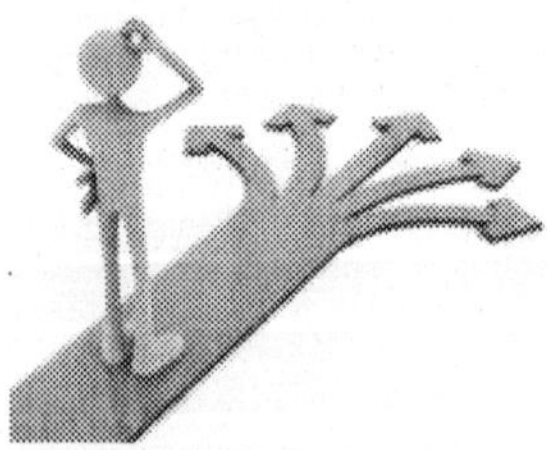

Whether a solution leads to a happy outcome such as a relationship reconciled, or an unhappy outcome such as a relationship ending, you need to live by it. Life isn't always about getting the answers you *want*, life is about getting the answers you *need*. Your *wants* can be misleading and often change, but your *needs* show who you really are.

Sometimes you may need to keep working on the problem until you find the right solution. In *The Amazing Results of Positive Thinking*, Peale emphasises how persistence is a very powerful force. He writes,

'Don't give up. It's amazing what simple persistence will do.'

Do not give up on the problem. If you persevere you will work out a solution. A solution can take time, you may require more information or you may need to ask for help. Seeking help can be a very important part of the solution. Always remember and believe you are worth helping.

If you feel stuck in a difficult problem seek help. Do not suffer alone needlessly. Seek help.

It may take time to apply the solution. Difficult problems can not be fixed instantly. You may need to work slowly toward incorporating the solution into your life. Applying the solution may require that you adjust to a new way of thinking or doing things.

Keep the balance

Assess your problem

Complete the checklist below to see if you are keeping your life in balance. Circle 'yes' or 'no'.

1. Are you looking at the problem in perspective with your life journey? Yes No

2. Do you keep in mind that your life journey will end one day? Yes No

3. Are you living by your personal laws? Yes No

4. Are your personal laws at the center of your life? Yes No

5. Are you willing to make a decision and apply it? Yes No

If you answered 'no' to any of the above questions you are not keeping your problems in perspective.

You need to move toward 'yes' to keep your life in balance. Using the Problem Solving Guide in Part 2 will help you.

A golfer and his buddies were playing golf for $1000 prize money to the winner. At the last hole, the lead golfer had a short putt to win the game and the prize. Even though it was a short putt, the golfer didn't want to be over confident, so he took his time to line up the putt. Just as he was about to swing, a funeral procession started to pass by. The golfer saw this and stopped. He put down his putter, took his hat off, bowed his head, and waited for the funeral procession to pass by.

After it passed, he picked up his putter, and hit the ball into the hole. He won the game and the money. While drinking at the bar, one of his buddies said, 'That was the most touching thing I have ever seen, the way you acted when that funeral procession went by. I can't believe you stopped playing at such a crucial point. You risked losing your concentration and missing the putt, just to pay your respects.' The golfer replied, 'Well, I was married to her for 25 years.'

PART 2

THE SOLUTION

HOUSTON, WE HAVE A SOLUTION.
JEFF LANG

CHAPTER 8

Problem Solving Guide

Use the Problem Solving Guide and you will reap the rewards.

A small effort is all it takes for the rewards to start flowing into your life.

JEFF LANG

This Problem Solving Guide will shake you out of any old negative thinking habits that are keeping you stuck in your problems.

It will help bring you to a point where what is wrong in your life can be made right.

> 'I truly believe that in every person's life there comes that moment in time when all things wrong can be made right.'
>
> Dr Phil
>
> (Dr Phillip McGraw)

NO
GUIDE
PROBLEM
SOLVING
GUIDE
Life
sucks!
Life is
great!
PROBLEMS

JEFF LANG

Why you need a guide

By using this **Problem Solving Guide**, you will develop the ability to 'act on' problems instead of simply 'reacting to' them.

Most people don't realize that their negative reactions often make matters worse.

Using negative coping techniques such as screaming and blaming are learnt behaviors. You can unlearn negative behaviors.

The **four simple tips** help you learn more empowering and positive coping techniques. This will increase your personal power – and increased personal power gives you inner strength. When you are strong on the inside, problems will not get you down.

MY WIFE HAS STOPPED NAGGING ME, IN FACT SHE HAS STOPPED TALKING TO ME.
HALF YOUR LUCK!
NO LUCK ABOUT IT, SHE HAS A VERY POWERFUL WEAPON-THE PEN. SHE WRITES NOTES AND LEAVES THEM ALL AROUND THE HOUSE-NOW I HAVE TO READ!
JEFF LANG

The Power of Writing

Just the physical act of writing stimulates the creative side of your brain and brings to light new thoughts and ideas about your problem.

Putting pen to paper helps you deal with problems and paves the way for the healing process to begin.

The process of writing is beneficial because it is the thinking that goes on, while you are writing, that makes the difference.

Your writing can be a freeing process, for when you discover what you are really thinking and feeling you will be on your way to finding solutions.

Using this **Problem Solving Guide** can set you on the path of healing from emotional hurts and in turn this will improve your physical wellbeing.

Problem Solving Guide

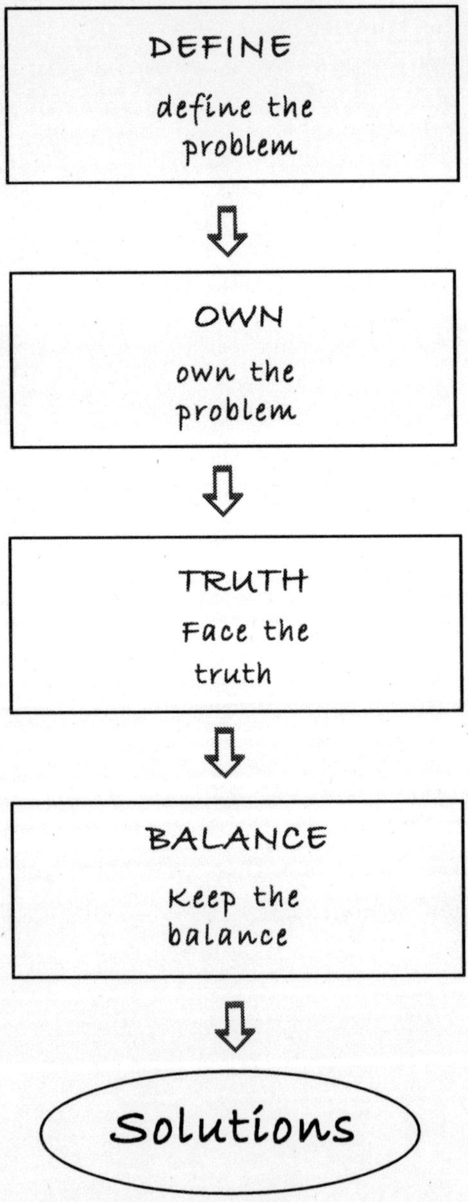

You can read or write

In using this **Problem Solving Guide**, you can either read the guide and answer the questions in your head or you can write down the answers.

Answering the questions will lead you to solutions.

Just write

In answering the questions, jot down notes or just a few words. Answer the questions as honestly as you can. The more you use this guide the better you will be at solving your problems. The better your problem solving skills the faster you will find solutions.

Take your time

Find a 'private and quiet' place, your mind works best when it is calm and relaxed. Take your time in answering the questions.

Expect emotions

When dealing with difficult problems, you may feel upset or even a little sad, while or after you write. Such emotions are natural and only temporary. They usually pass within a short time. After they have passed, you will feel a sense of relief and happiness.

Keep it private

Keep your writing 'strictly private' – for your eyes only. You need to feel completely free to express your deepest thoughts and true feelings. This enables you to get to the heart of any problem.

Helpful Questions

The *Problem Solving Guide* gives you helpful questions. When you approach problems with helpful questions, you find better answers.

Answering the questions is important. It is the thinking that goes on while you are answering that makes a difference and reveals solutions to you.

Depending on the problem some questions will have more impact than others. All the questions are designed to help you work out what you can do for yourself.

DEFINE TIP

DEFINE
to
Understand

Problems need to be
examined correctly to
find the right solution.

Define the problem

Write down words or just answer the questions in your head.

Define Tip

When you define a problem correctly
you are halfway to the solution.

'Dr Phil'

Title your problem

E.g. *John and I argue everyday.*

....

....

....

Silence and calm

Are you in a quiet, private place? This is the best setting for dealing with problems.

Take five long, deep breaths. Close your eyes as you inhale and exhale. This will help reduce your stress and calm your mind.

Focus on what you are grateful for in your life today. Think of what makes you happy as this will increase your personal power.

Diagnose the problem: Write down the facts of the situation. You can deal with your feelings later.

For example – *John yells at me. He doesn't listen to me. He refuses to talk.*

Describe the problem and break it down.

Don't just write about the facts that suit you. Look at all the facts, especially the facts you don't want to admit to yourself.

For example – *I yell at John. I bring up the past. I use hurtful words. I criticize and belittle him.*

How am I part of the problem?

Look at the facts first, so you can examine the problem correctly.

Type of Problems		Personal Power
Direct control Problems involving you only *e.g. bad habits, addiction, depression.*	⇨	Your personal power lies in changing your beliefs and behavior.
Indirect control Problems involving another person *e.g. partner, children, boss, friends, family.*	⇨	Your personal power lies in changing your attitude toward them. *Seek to first understand ... then to be understood.*
No control Problems involving the past or life events *e.g. earthquake, storm, childhood, death.*	⇨	Your personal power lies in changing your way of thinking.

Type of problem: Can you identify the type your problem is? In which category does it belong: *direct control*, *indirect control* or *no control?* (See box on previous page for guidance.)

Write down the category in which your problem belongs.

The type of my problem is:

....

Where does your personal power lie?
(See box on previous page for guidance.)

My personal power lies in:

....

....

....

....

Identify the real issue: Often problems are expressed as topics, for example, 'you were *rude* to me', 'you *spend* too much', 'you *lied* to me', when the real issue isn't recognized, such as below:

Common Topics *(surface)*	Real Issues *(underlying)*
spending	control
lies	trust
abuse	power
neglect	love
jealousy	insecurity
rudeness	respect
misbehaving	discipline

For example:

You can't solve money problems with more money – why? Because it is about control.

If you can't control your money (i.e. your spending) on a $50,000 income, you will not be able to control your spending on a $1,000,000 income.

Write down the topic of your problem. Then see if you can identify the real issue.

The topic of my problem is:

....

....

The real issue of my problem is:

....

....

To identify the real issue, ask yourself 'what are my feelings telling me?'

Realize your thoughts: Are you blaming the problem for making you feel unhappy?

You need to realize that *your negative thoughts* are making you unhappy, not the problem.

You can not always control your problems, but you always have control of your thoughts.

Being able to control your negative thoughts increases your personal power.

What negative thoughts are making me unhappy about my problem?

Your thoughts create your feelings.
Your feelings create your life.

Express your feelings: Really think about your feelings and use words to express yourself freely.

Say exactly how you feel, such as – sad, angry, hurt, regretful, upset, disappointed, frustrated, confused, afraid, etc.

Negative feelings will block your personal power. You need to release them.

Express any negative feelings that your problem may be causing you. Say this out loud to yourself to release any pent-up emotions.

What negative feelings do I have about my problem?

Suppressing your feelings will only bring you more pain. You need to give your feelings a voice.

Write to heal: The release that writing offers can help you begin to heal from the pain of problems and this will increase your personal power.

Write down helpful thoughts that will make you feel better, such as – what you are grateful for, what you appreciate about a person, the good times in your life. This will shift your thinking.

What am I grateful for in my life today?

Gratitude and appreciation are the
ways for the healing to begin.

Learn from the problem: It is easy to only see the negative side of your problem. However, each problem is sending you a message about your life. What is it?

Find the value of every problem. Learning from a problem will increase your personal power.

Write down what you can learn about yourself or your life from this problem.

Do you need to be more forgiving, to be more understanding, to be more accepting, to change your attitude, to make better choices?

What is good about my problem?

What can I learn from my problem?

Helpful thoughts are more powerful
than negative thoughts.

OWN

TIP

OWN

means

power

Own your problems and
you will have the power
to solve them.

Own the problem

If a problem affects you,
then it's your problem.

Own Tip

Taking responsibility means never blaming anyone else for anything you are being, doing having or feeling.

Susan Jeffers

Own gives you power

When you own the problem and take 100% responsibility for it, you will have 100% power to find a solution.

You always have personal power.

You have the power to change your thinking, to change your reaction and to seek help if you are stuck.

If you say 'I can't do anything about my problems', you are trying to get out of your responsibility.

Stop blaming others: If you are blaming others or circumstances for your problem – stop now.

When it comes to dealing with problems, the harsh reality is that 'life is not fair'. This reality is the same for everyone.

Blaming only makes you a victim and weakens your personal power.

Am I blaming others or circumstances for my problem? If so, who or what am I blaming?

Write out the following sentence:

Blaming only makes me a victim. I will stop blaming [insert name] and focus on looking for solutions.

Stop acting like a victim.
Stop blaming other people.

Stop blaming yourself: If you are blaming yourself for your problem – stop now.

When it comes to dealing with problems, just accept that you are human and that all humans make mistakes.

Blaming yourself only makes you a victim and weakens your personal power.

Am I blaming myself for my problem?

If so, why am I blaming myself?

Write out the following sentence:

I will stop blaming myself, it only makes me a victim. I will seek to learn more so I can do better in the future. I will focus on looking for solutions.

Stop making yourself a victim.
Stop blaming yourself.

Fight criticism and defeat: Protect yourself from hurtful thoughts.

Only you have control of your *self-talk – the words you say to yourself.*

Only accept words that will build you up. Reject words that bring you down and make you feel bad about yourself.

Hurtful self-criticism and self-defeat will weaken your personal power. Fight against them.

What words of self-criticism or self-defeat am I saying to myself about my problem?

Write out the following sentence:

This problem is only temporary, I will find a solution. I will be okay.

Say 'NO' to hurtful self-criticism and self-defeat.

Stop making excuses: If you are making excuses for not dealing with your problem – stop now.

Excuses only keep you stuck in the problem.

If you are stuck then you need help.

Your task is to focus all your efforts on getting help. Seeking help will strengthen your personal power.

Examples of excuses

- *I should break off this relationship, but I don't want to be alone.*
- *I should get out of debt, but I can't stop myself from spending.*
- *I should quit smoking but it's too hard, I am addicted.*
- *I want to lose weight, but junk food makes me feel better.*

What excuses am I making for not dealing with or for putting up with my problem?

What is one small change I can make? e.g. speak to someone.

Get out of the excuses trap!

Face the pain: Learn to deal with the pain of problems.

Dealing with pain isn't easy, but you can do it. When you face the pain, problems can be resolved and the pain goes away.

If you don't push through the fear of pain, the pain will always remain.

Fearing pain is worse than going through the pain.

Are you focusing on what you don't want? Ask yourself, 'What am I afraid of – being hurt, failure, loneliness, loss, rejection?'

Focus on what you want. What do I want for myself? This will help you deal with the pain.

Keep focusing on what you want.

TRUTH

TIP

TRUTH
reveals
solutions

Solutions can only be found from the truth.

Face the truth

Not facing the truth
will keep you stuck
in the problem.

Truth Tip

And you will know the truth, and
the truth will make you free.

John 8:32

One truth that you must face – no excuses, no buts, no denials – is that you play a role in all your problems. This means:

You are part of the problem.

While this may not sound like good news, it actually is because it also means:

You are part of the solution.

Facing the truth is more than just saying:

- *yes, I have a problem.*

Facing the truth is also about asking yourself,

- *what am I doing?*
- *what am I believing?*
- *what am I not doing?*
- *what am I putting up with?*

... *that has caused this problem.*

Consider the following question:

(Circle answer)

Am I being totally honest and admitting the truth to myself? **Yes** **No**

If you answered 'yes' to this question you will find the solution to your problems.

Check your beliefs are true.

Your beliefs are fixed thoughts you have accepted as true.

You need to realize that – not all your thoughts are actually true. Some thoughts are false.

False thoughts may be repeating in your mind and have become false beliefs.

False beliefs are thoughts that feel true, but if you look at them more closely you will see they are false. (See next page for examples.)

(Circle answer)

Will I check my thoughts are true?	**Yes**	**No**
Will I change any false beliefs?	**Yes**	**No**

You need to answer 'yes' to the above questions if you want to find a solution to your problems.

Common false beliefs

False belief

My way is right, they are wrong.

True belief

What is right for me may not be right for someone else. We are all different.

False belief

I can't lose weight, I have no will power.

True belief

I can lose weight. Losing weight is not about will power. It is about changing my habits. I can slowly replace bad food habits with good food habits.

False belief

My partner should try to make me happy.

True belief

It is my job to make me happy, it is not my partner's job.

Are my beliefs true? What am I believing about this problem? (Take a close look at your beliefs and write them down.)

Check for false beliefs – am I holding on to any false beliefs? Write them down.

False beliefs come from false thinking.

Below are ten common false thinking traps.

Are you being affected by any of the false thoughts below? Circle 'Yes' or 'No'.

False thinking traps

False thinking traps		
▪ black and white thinking	Yes	No
▪ unrealistic expectations	Yes	No
▪ selective thinking	Yes	No
▪ overgeneralizing	Yes	No
▪ exaggerating	Yes	No
▪ catastrophizing	Yes	No
▪ personalizing	Yes	No
▪ jumping to conclusions	Yes	No
▪ mistaking feelings for facts	Yes	No
▪ thinking life should be fair	Yes	No

(Find out more about these 'false thinking traps' on pages 70-71.)

Identify false thinking: If you answered 'yes' to any of the false thinking traps on the previous page, write them down below.

What is my false thinking?

....

....

....

....

What am I saying to myself that is making me believe my false thinking.

....

....

....

....

....

Focus on helpful thinking: Challenge your false thinking.

This is not just about replacing negative thoughts with positive thoughts. Which can be difficult.

It is about checking to make sure that your thoughts are rational, helpful and true.

> **Your aim is to challenge your false thinking and replace it with helpful thinking.**

For example:

False thinking: *I am just a loser and always fail at everything!*

Helpful thinking: *Everyone wins and loses, succeeds and fails, no one is just a winner or just a loser.*

What can I say to myself to change my false thoughts to helpful thoughts?

See the next page for some examples.

Change your false thoughts by focusing on helpful thoughts.

Here are some helpful thoughts to inspire you to create you own.

Mistakes happen, nobody is perfect,
I will choose to forgive.

My thoughts don't control my life,
I can change my thoughts, I control
my life.

I can ride this problem out and not
let it get to me. It is only temporary.

My negative feelings will not kill me,
these feelings will pass. No feeling
lasts forever.

This problem sucks, but I am strong
and I can deal with it.

I can be anxious and still deal with
this problem.

I can learn to cope with my fears. Let
fear be a counsellor not a prisoner.

Check your perception is true.

Your perception is how you see a problem.

This needs to be true and accurate.

If your perception is based on *false beliefs* and *bad past experiences*, then you are seeing your problem in a false way.

(Circle answer)

Will I check my perception? **Yes** **No**

Will I change false perceptions? **Yes** **No**

You need to answer 'yes' to the above questions if you want to find a solution to your problems.

The questions on the following pages will help you check if your perception is true.

Is my perception true?

Below are the four common false perceptions that distort how you see your problem.

Are you being affected by any of the false perceptions below? Circle 'Yes' or 'No'.

False Perceptions

▪ Past events affect how I live today.	Yes	No
▪ Other people cause me to react.	Yes	No
▪ Life events control me.	Yes	No
▪ I can not change.	Yes	No

(Find out more about these 'false perceptions' on pages 76-79.)

How am I seeing my problem? Are you being affected by any of the false perceptions on the previous page ? Write down which ones.

.... 

....

....

....

....

....

....

....

....

You do not react to events.
You react to your thinking
(perception) about the event.

You may not have been responsible for what happened to you in the past, but you are responsible for how you act now.

False perceptions stop you from finding solutions.

Seeing your problem through false perceptions distorts your view of reality and this can make matters worse.

(Find out more about these 'false perceptions' on pages 80.)

How can I see my problem differently?
(See examples below.)

I have the power to change my perception.

- I will stop living in the past.
- I am responsible for my reactions.
- I have control of my thoughts no matter what happens in life.
- I choose how I want to be and I can change when I need to.

The Truth Questions

Ask better questions and you will get better answers to your problems.

Asking better questions increases your personal power and you will find solutions faster.

With increased personal power you will feel better about yourself and your life.

Answer the following **Truth Questions** and you will see the path towards a solution more clearly.

1. What am I *thinking* that is contributing to the problem?

Try first to understand ...
then to be understood.

Learn to be a perceiver rather than a judger – judging too quickly can lead you to wrong thinking. Are you judging yourself or are you judging others?

Move toward what you want.

What was done to you in the past is not your fault, but what you are doing now is your choice.

Avoid living in the past and making life decisions based on fear.

To move forward in your life, make decisions on what you need and what you want now.

2. What am I *doing* that is contributing to this problem?

Are my actions making the problem worse? What actions can I take that could make things better?

You teach people how to treat you.

Are the people in your life treating you with dignity and respect?

If someone is not, you need to face this fact and stand up for yourself or move on without them.

If you want the best in life, seek it and do not settle for less.

You need to give respect and be respected by others.

You need to be your own best friend.

3. What am I *allowing* that is contributing to the problem?

How am I letting others treat me? How am I treating myself?

Forgiveness is a choice; it is not a feeling.

Have you been hurt by others?

Are you still saying to yourself that you will never forgive them?

If you hold on to feelings of hatred and anger, you are only hurting yourself.

Negative feelings change who you are and steal your joy. **You can't hurt another person with bitter thoughts, you only hurt yourself.**

Forgiveness is not about saying what someone did was okay.

It is about saying 'I free myself from you'.

Forgiveness is not easy, but it will release you from the feelings of hurt and anger.

Understand that forgiveness is for you.

4. What am I *saying* that is contributing to the problem?

Am I being part of the solution or am I being part of the problem?

Deal with your pain.

If you are struggling with feelings of hurt, you need to 'ride the storm'.

These feelings will go away because all feelings change, no feeling is forever.

Avoid numbing your feelings with alcohol or drugs.

Reach out to someone you can trust, such as your religious leader, local doctor, therapist, a valued family member or a friend. Seek help to heal.

5. What am I *being* that is contributing to the problem?

Am I being a victim? What can I do to help myself deal with the pain?

Create the life you deserve.

If there is something that is not working in your life you need to do something about it.

If you are dealing with a problem you cannot handle alone, you need to put all your effort into getting help.

You are worth helping! Sometimes the solution to your problem can only be found by getting help when you are stuck.

6. What am I *not doing* that is contributing to the problem?

Do I need to ask for help? Who can I ask for help? Am I looking for information to learn more about my problem? Where can I look for information?

Do a reality check

Avoid measuring your self-worth according to what other people say about you. The truth is – 'I am okay'.

Self-hate and hating others cannot lead to solutions. Only self-love and forgiveness lead to solutions.

Try your 'daily affirmation' when you are struggling with problems. See next page.

You need to reprogram negative and hurtful self-talk into helpful self-talk. Only you can control your thoughts.

If you feel bad about yourself
you cannot deal with problems.

Feeling good about yourself
will lead to solutions.

Your daily affirmation

I am OKAY

I love myself with my faults and mistakes, because no one is perfect.

I love others with their faults and forgive their mistakes, because no one is perfect.

BALANCE TIP

BALANCE
gives
perspective

Learn to live
with problems,
not in problems.

Keep the balance

Look at your problems in the context of your life journey.

Balance Tip

Your life journey will end one day. Ask yourself:

'Am I letting this problem spoil my journey?'

If you become stuck on a problem and live in a problem, you will lose perspective and your life will be out of balance.

Problems are a part of life. You need to learn to live *with* problems, not live *in* problems.

The key to keeping your problems in perspective is to have a strong and stable sense of who you are and what your values are.

Your personal laws: By knowing who you are and what values you want to live by, you form your own personal laws. For example:

My personal laws:

- spend less than I earn.
- choose to forgive and move on.
- listen first before responding.
- avoid wanting to always be right.
- spend time with loved ones.
- pursue my hopes and dreams.
- pay attention to my feelings.
- take care of my health.

Your personal laws should protect, respect and serve you. They help keep your life in balance and problems in perspective with your life journey.

Imagine, for a moment, if there were no laws in society: life would be chaos without rules and guidelines for people to live by.

You need to know your personal laws and live by them.

If you don't, when difficult problems arise, your life will be in chaos because you have no guidelines to follow.

Your personal laws are your guide that help you navigate through the problems in life. (For more about 'personal laws' go to pages 89-90.)

Consider the following questions:

(Circle answer)

Do I know what my personal laws are?

Yes No

Am I living by my personal laws?

Yes No

If you answered 'yes' to the above questions you will be able to keep your problems in perspective with your life journey.

If you answered 'no' see page 90 for more personal law examples.

Your personal laws need to be at the center of your life – this is the only part of your life you have control over.

If you are money-centered, children-centered, partner-centered or career-centered then you are vulnerable to problems with that person or object which you can't control.

While other areas of your life can change at any moment, your personal laws can only be changed by you.

Find out more about being 'personal laws' centered on pages 92-94.)

Which personal law does my problem affect? *e.g choose to forgive and move on.*

....

....

....

....

....

Your reaction: Are you being true to your 'personal laws' or have you become too 'emotional' about your problem?

Relying on your 'personal laws' instead of your 'emotions' will increase your personal power and help you solve problems more effectively.

Write down your 'emotional' reaction and compare it to your 'personal laws' reaction.

My 'emotional' reaction to the problem:

(e.g. hating someone for hurting me)

....

....

....

....

....

My 'personal laws' reaction to the problem:

(e.g. choosing to forgive them and move on with my life)

....

....

....

....

....

....

The next time a problem occurs, how would I like to react?

What helpful self-talk could I say to myself for next time? (See next page.)

Examples of helpful self-talk

- I will be a peace maker and not get so caught up with being right all the time.
- I need to stop living in the past. I will forgive and move on with my life.
- I will respect other people's decisions, even if I do not always agree with them.
- I did the best I could with what I knew; I will seek to know more so I can do better.
- I have already been through other painful experiences and I have survived.
- This problem sucks, but I'm strong and I can deal with it.
- These are my feelings now, but feelings always change, they will eventually go away.

(See pages 72-73 for more examples.)

Your perspective: How old are you now? Imagine yourself at 100 years old, relaxing and reflecting on your life experiences.

What advice would I give to myself about this problem if I were 100 years old?

Am I letting this problem spoil my life journey?

If you answered 'yes', write the following:

I will continue to enjoy my life journey. I am grateful for the good things in my life. I will seek to be happy while I am working toward a solution to my problem.

Your decision: With any problem the solution lies in using your personal power. You have the power to change your thinking, to change your reaction, and to get help. **The solution always lies within you.**

Write down all the solutions you can think of. The aim is to get your brain thinking about all your options and to get the ideas flowing.

Look at the different solutions. What is the best one? Remember – 'the only person I can control or change is me'.

What steps will I take to apply the solution? What can I do starting from today?

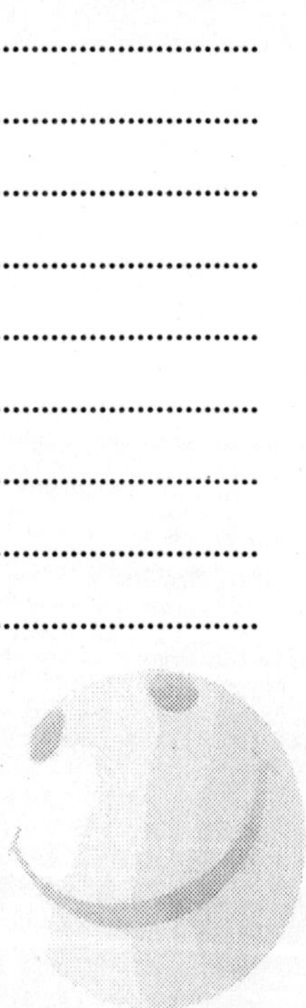

MAKING A DECISION

You may be afraid of making a wrong decision. This fear can stop you from moving forward in your life.

Instead of looking at a decision as being either right or wrong, look at a decision as different life paths you can follow.

Making one decision will put you on path A; making another decision puts you on path B.

While you cannot always be sure you have made the best decision, you can always decide to make the best of your decision.

FACING THE TRUTH

The most common reason for problems not being solved is that the truth has not been admitted. Check that you have faced the truth about your problem. If you are not totally honest with yourself, you will not find a solution.

SOLUTIONS TAKE TIME

Applying a solution to some problems can take time. There are no quick fixes for difficult problems. Give the solution time to work. If you can see positive results emerging, then your solution is working.

SETBACKS WILL OCCUR

When applying a solution, you may fall back into negative thinking or old bad habits. Problem solving isn't about being perfect, it is about moving in the right direction. Keep focusing on the solution and expect setbacks. Pick yourself up and move forward with your solution.

Setbacks will occur. That is okay.
Keep moving forward with your solution
if you can see any improvements.

If my chosen solution did not work, why do I think it didn't work?

If my solution did not work, what can I do next?

- Apply another solution from page 194.
- Use Problem Solving Guide again.
- Seek help with this problem.

What will I do next?

For example – I will seek help; I will learn more about my problem; I will talk to a trusted friend, my doctor or my church leader; I will check I have faced the truth.

Check your use of the *four simple tips*. Tick the checklist below.

Tip 1 – define

- ☐ Do you know what *type* the problem is?
- ☐ Did you give your *feelings* a voice?
- ☐ Are you taking the *time* to work on the problem?

Tip 2 – own

- ☐ Have you *owned* the problem?
- ☐ Are you *taking responsibility* for your actions?
- ☐ Are you willing to look *within yourself* for the solution?

Tip 3 – truth

☐ Are you facing the truth about the *role you play* in the problem?

☐ Are you willing to put all your *beliefs* and *perceptions* up for review?

☐ Have you asked yourself the *truth questions* and answered them truthfully?

☐ If you are stuck, are you *seeking help*?

Tip 4 – balance

☐ Are you looking at the problem in *perspective* with your life journey?

☐ Is your life centered on your *personal laws*, instead of being people- or object-centered?

☐ Are you willing to make a *decision* and *act* on it?

Keep Trying!

Persistence is a very powerful force. Keep working on your problems. If you persevere you will work out solutions to them.

Realize also that getting help can be a very important part of solving difficult problems. You are not alone. Everyone has problems; so don't suffer alone. It is never too late to reach out for help. You are worth helping!

Visit our Website

www.noproblembook.com

See our website for information on references and resources you can use to help you get back on track with solving problems and increase your personal power. When you know better ... you can do better.

You can email Elizabeth Hanley at
elizabeth@noproblembook.com

About the Author

Elizabeth Hanley's career as a Senior Reference Librarian spanned work in corporate, educational and public libraries. She has a Post Graduate Diploma in Library and Information Science from the University of Technology, Australia. Her skills in helping people find information for their problems have led to the writing of this book.

As a librarian with access to thousands of books, Elizabeth used her researching skills to analyze what experts and best-selling self-help authors wrote about problem solving, such as Dr Phil, Stephen Covey, Anthony Robbins, Susan Jeffers, Dale Carnegie and many more.

From reading hundreds of books on the subject Elizabeth grouped the best advice given under **four simple tips**. From these tips she formed a clear-cut **problem solving guide** to assist her in her own life and to assist others.

Elizabeth has discovered the joy of having a ***No Problem!*** life and hopes that you will too.

References

Carlson, Richard. *Don't Sweat the Small Stuff and it's all small stuff*, Bantam Books, Sydney, 1997, p. 45.

Carlson, Richard. *What About the Big Stuff?* Harper Collins, Sydney, 2002, p. 3.

Carlson, Richard. *You Can Be Happy No Matter What*, Bantam Books, Sydney, 1997.

Carnegie, Dale. *How to Win Friends and Influence People*, Harper Business, Sydney, 1999.

Carnegie, Dale. *How to Stop Worrying and Start Living*, Vermilion, London, 1992.

Covey, Stephen R. T*he 7 Habits of Highly Effective People*, Fireside Books, Sydney, 1990, pp. 71, 86, 108.

Edelman, Sarah. *Change Your Thinking*, ABC Books, Sydney, 2002.

Hay, Louise L. *You Can Heal Your Life*, Hay House, Sydney, 2004.

Hill, Napoleon. *Think and Grow Rich,* Classic Books, Australia, 2005. p. 80.

Jeffers, Susan. *Feel the Fear and Do It Anyway*, Vermilion, London, 1991, p. 52.

McGraw, Phillip C. *Life Strategies*, Vermilion, London, 1999, pp. 57, 63, 153.

Murphy, Joseph. *The Power of Your Subconscious Mind*, Pocket Books, Sydney, 2000.

Peale, Norman Vincent. *The Amazing Results of Positive Thinking*, Vermilion, London, 1992, pp. 163, 169.

Peale, Norman Vincent. *The Power of Positive Thinking*, Vermilion, London, 1990.

Peck, M. Scott. *The Road Less Traveled*, Rider, Sydney, 2003, pp. 3, 4.

Rankin, Petra. *Fast Track Your Success & Happiness*, Brief Books, South Australia, 2005.

Ratcliffe, Gail. *Take Control of Your Life*, Finch, Sydney, 2003.

Richardson, Pam. *The Life Coach*, Hamlyn, London, 2004.

Robbins, Anthony. *Awaken the Giant Within*, Pocket Books, Sydney, 1991, pp. 179, 180, 187.

Robbins, Anthony. *Unlimited Power*, Pocket Books, Sydney, 2001.

Spencer, Rita & Rossmanith, Angela. *Stop Struggling*, Angus & Robertson, Sydney, 1995.

No Problem! titles

No Problem! Problem Solving Guide

This is the companion book to *No Problem! how to focus on solutions.* It is the practical, easy to read, step-by-step guide on how you can work through problems to form viable solutions.

No Problem! Problem Solving Guide on CD

This is an easy-to-use, practical CD that you can either read by itself, or fill in on your computer. It guides you step-by-step to help you form viable solutions to your problems.